PIANO | VOCAL | GUITAR

40 MOST STREAMED SONGS
OF 2017-20

ISBN 978-1-5400-3568-4

HAL•LEONARD®

Visit Hal Leonard Online at
www.halleonard.com

Contact Us:
Hal Leonard
7777 West Bluemound Road
Milwaukee, WI 53213
Email: info@halleonard.com

In Europe contact:
Hal Leonard Europe Limited
42 Wigmore Street
Marylebone, London, W1U 2RN
Email: info@halleonardeurope.com

In Australia contact:
Hal Leonard Australia Pty. Ltd.
4 Lentara Court
Cheltenham, Victoria, 3192 Australia
Email: info@halleonard.com.au

CONTENTS

CHAINED TO THE RHYTHM

Words and Music by KATY PERRY,
MAX MARTIN, SIA FURLER,
ALI PAYAMI and SKIP MARLEY

Moderate Dance Pop

Are we cra - zy? Liv-ing our ___ lives through ___ a lens. ___

Trapped in our ___ white pick - et fence ___ like or -

BELIEVER

Words and Music by DAN REYNOLDS,
WAYNE SERMON, BEN McKEE,
DANIEL PLATZMAN, JUSTIN TRANTOR,
MATTIAS LARSSON and ROBIN FREDRICKSSON

First things first: I'm - a say all the words in-side my head. I'm fired up and
Sec-ond things sec-ond: don't you tell me what you think that I can be. I'm the one at the

tired of the way that things have been, oh, ooh, ___ the way that things have
sail, I'm the mas-ter of my sea, oh, ooh, ___ the mas-ter of my

been, oh, ooh. ___
sea, oh, ooh. ___ I was

*Recorded a half step higher.

DUSK TILL DAWN

Words and Music by ZAYN MALIK,
SIA FURLER and GREG KURSTIN

FEEL IT STILL

Words and Music by JOHN GOURLEY,
ZACH CAROTHERS, JASON SECHRIST,
ERIC HOWK, KYLE O'QUIN, BRIAN HOLLAND,
FREDDIE GORMAN, GEORGIA DOBBINS,
ROBERT BATEMAN, WILLIAM GARRETT,
JOHN HILL and ASA TACCONE

lit - tle ba - by girl is in need. ___ Am I com - ing out - ta left field?

Ooh, ___ I'm a reb - el just for kicks, now. I've been feel - ing it since

nine - teen six - ty - six, now.
{Might be o - ver ___ now, but I feel it still.}
{Might have had your ___ fill, but you feel it still.}

Ooh, ___ I'm a

DESPACITO

Words and Music by LUIS FONSI,
ERIKA ENDER, JUSTIN BIEBER, JASON BOYD,
MARTY JAMES GARTON and RAMÓN AYALA

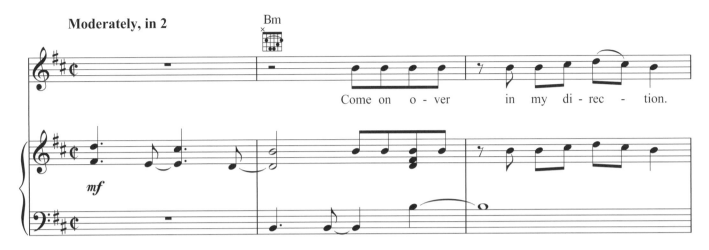

Come on o-ver in my di-rec - tion.

So thank-ful for that, it's such a bless - in', ___ yeah. Turn ev-'ry sit-u-

a - tion in-to heav - en, ___ yeah. Oh, ___ oh, ___ you ___ are ___

-do, pa-ra que te a-cuer-des si no es-tás con-mi-go.

Des - pa - ci - to. Quie-ro des-nu-dar-te a be-sos des-pa-ci-

-to, fir-mo en las pa-re-des de tu la-be-rin - to, y ha-cer de tu

cuer-po to-do un ma-nu-scri - to. _____

FRIENDS

Words and Music by ANNE-MARIE NICHOLSON,
NATALIE MAREE DUNN, MARSHMELLO,
EDEN ANDERSON, SARAH BLANCHARD,
PABLO BOWMAN, RICHARD BOARDMAN
and JASMINE THOMPSON

IT AIN'T ME

Words and Music by ALI TAMPOSI,
SELENA GOMEZ, ANDREW WOTMAN,
KYRRE GØRVELL-DAHLL and BRIAN LEE

HAVANA

Words and Music by CAMILA CABELLO, LOUIS BELL,
PHARRELL WILLIAMS, ADAM FEENEY, ALI TAMPOSI,
BRIAN LEE, ANDREW WOTMAN, BRITTANY HAZZARD,
JEFFERY LAMAR WILLIAMS and KAAN GUNESBERK

CODA

N.C.

van - a, Ha - van - a, ooh na na. *(See additional lyrics)*

Gm   E♭   D7   Gm   E♭   D7

N.C.   Gm   E♭   D7

Gm   E♭maj7   D7   Gm   E♭   D7

Additional Lyrics

Jeffery.
Just graduated, fresh on campus, mmm.
Fresh out East Atlanta with no manners, damn.
Fresh out East Atlanta.
Bump on her bumper like a traffic jam (jam).
Hey, I was quick to pay that girl like Uncle Sam. (Here you go, ay).
Back it on me, shawty cravin' on me.
Get to diggin' on me (on me).
She waited on me. (Then what?)
Shawty cakin' on me, got the bacon on me. (Wait up.)
This is history in the makin' on me (on me).
Point blank, close range, that be.
If it cost a million, that's me (that's me).
I was gettin' mula, man, they feel me.

I DON'T WANNA LIVE FOREVER

(Fifty Shades Darker)

from FIFTY SHADES DARKER

Words and Music by TAYLOR SWIFT,
JACK ANTONOFF and SAM DEW

Easy Pop feel

Oh, _____ oh, oh, oh, _____ oh. _____

Oh, _____ oh, oh, oh, _____ oh. _____

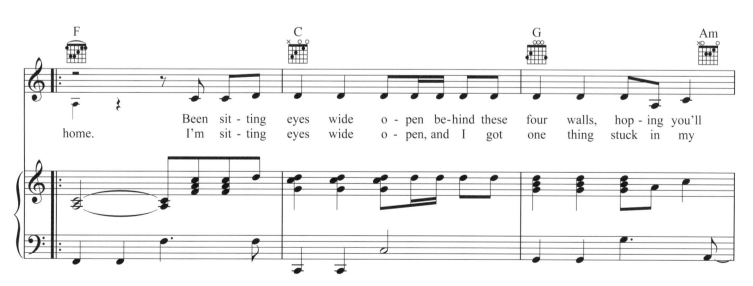

home. Been sit-ting eyes wide o-pen be-hind these four walls, hop-ing you'll

I'm sit-ting eyes wide o-pen, and I got one thing stuck in my

I FEEL IT COMING

Words and Music by ABEL TESFAYE,
ERIC CHEDEVILLE, GUY-MANUEL DE HOMEM-CHRISTO,
THOMAS BANGALTER, HENRY WALTER
and MARTIN McKINNEY

Tell me what you real-ly like. ___

Ba-by, I can take my time. ___
so, ba-by, this the per-fect time. ___

We don't ev-er have to fight. ___
I'm just try'n' to get you high, ___

I'M THE ONE

Words and Music by NICHOLAS MATTHEW BALDING, JASON BOYD,
BOBBY CLIFTON BRACKINS, RAY JACOBS, KHALED KHALED,
DWAYNE CARTER, QUAVIOUS KEYATE MARSHALL,
CHANCELOR JONATHAN BENNETT, JUSTIN BIEBER
and DAVID PARK

ISSUES

Words and Music by BENJAMIN LEVIN,
MIKKEL ERIKSEN, TOR HERMANSEN,
JULIA MICHAELS and JUSTIN TRANTER

LET YOU DOWN

Words and Music by TOMMEE PROFITT
and NATE FEUERSTEIN

Rap 1: (See additional lyrics)
Rap 2: (See additional lyrics)

Feels like we're on the edge right __ now. __ I wish that I could

say I'm __ proud. __ I'm sor - ry that I let you __ down, __ I - l -

Additional Lyrics

Rap 1: I guess I'm a disappointment. Doin' everything I can, I don't wanna make you disappointed.
It's annoying. I just wanna make you feel like everything I ever did wasn't ever tryin' to make an issue for you.
But I guess the more you thought about everything, you were never even wrong in the first place, right?
Yeah, I'm-a just ignore you. Walkin' towards you with my head down, lookin' at the ground. I'm embarrassed for you.
Paranoia, what did I do wrong this time? That's parents for you. Very loyal? Should-a had my back, but you put a knife in it.
My hands are full. What else should I carry for you? I care for you, but...

Rap 2: You don't wanna make this work, you just wanna make this worse. Want me to listen to you, but you don't ever hear my words.
You don't wanna know my hurt yet. Let me guess; you want an apology probably. How can we keep goin' at a rate like this?
We can't, so I guess I'm-a have to leave. Please don't come after me. I just wanna be alone right now.
I don't really wanna think at all. Go ahead, just drink it off. Both know you're gonna call tomorrow like nothin's wrong.
Ain't that what you always do? I feel like every time I talk to you, you're in an awful mood. What else can I offer you?
There's nothing left right now. I gave it all to you.

Rap 3: Don't talk down to me. That's not gonna work now. Packed all my clothes and I moved out.
I don't even wanna go to your house. Every time I sit on that couch, I feel like you lecture me.
Eventually, I bet that we could-a made this work and probably would-a figured things out. But I guess I'm a letdown.
But it's cool, I checked out. Oh, you wanna be friends now? Okay, let's put my fake face on and pretend now.
Sit around and talk about the good times that didn't even happen. I mean, why you laughin'?
Must have missed that joke. Let me see if I can find a reaction. No, but at least you're happy.

LOOK WHAT YOU MADE ME DO

Words and Music by TAYLOR SWIFT,
JACK ANTONOFF, RICHARD FAIRBRASS,
FRED FAIRBRASS and ROB MANZOLI

Lyrics:

I don't like your lit-tle games, don't like your tilt-ed
I don't like your per-fect crime, how you laugh when you

stage. The role you made me play of the fool. No, I don't like you.
lie. You said the gun was mine. Is-n't cool. No, I

To Coda ⊕

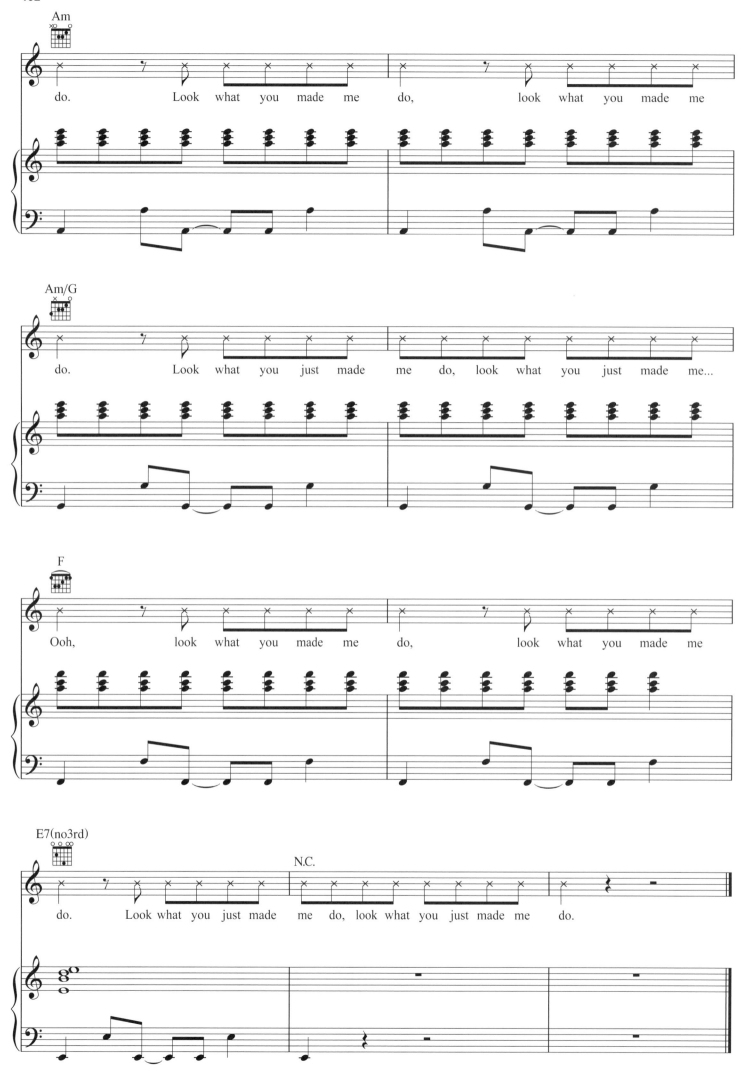

MEANT TO BE

Words and Music by BLETA REXHA,
JOSH MILLER, TYLER HUBBARD
and DAVID GARCIA

MALIBU

Words and Music by OREN YOEL
and MILEY CYRUS

* *Vocal written an octave higher than sung.*

114

NEW RULES

Words and Music by CAROLINE AILIN,
IAN KIRKPATRICK and EMILY WARREN SCHWARTZ

PARIS

Words and Music by ANDREW TAGGART,
KRISTOFFER ERIKSSON and FREDRIK HAEGGSTAM

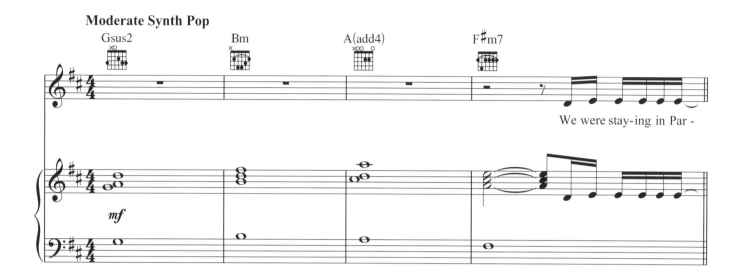

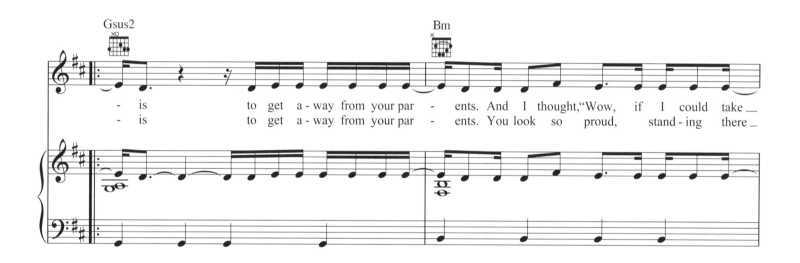

show them we are bet-ter. We were stay-ing in Par - is.

Let's

show them we are bet-ter.

Let's

NO TEARS LEFT TO CRY

Words and Music by ARIANA GRANDE,
SAVAN KOTECHA, MAX MARTIN
and ILYA

Atmospherically

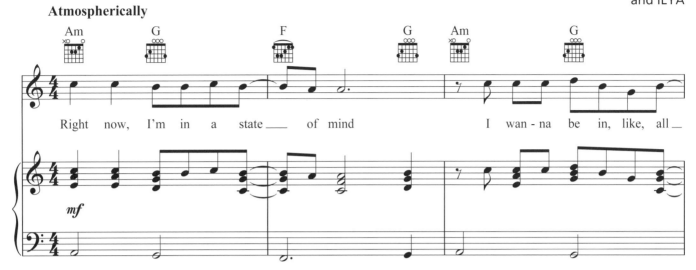

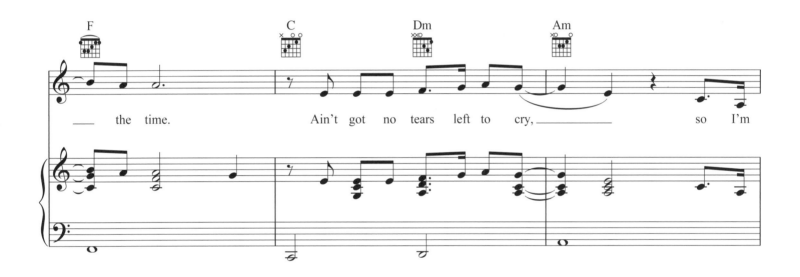

Faster, with a groove

PERFECT

Words and Music by
ED SHEERAN

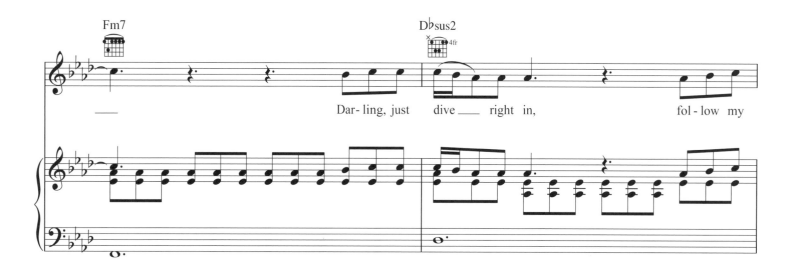

PSYCHO

Words and Music by LOUIS BELL,
TYRONE WILLIAM GRIFFIN JR., AUSTIN POST
and CARL ROSEN

jean, still in my Vans though. All V - V - S - es put you in a neck - lace. Girl, you look

D.S. al Coda

beau - ti - ful to - night. Stars on the roof, they match - ing with the jew'l - ry.
Damn, my A - P go - in'

CODA

friend when I'm roll - in' through my end zone.

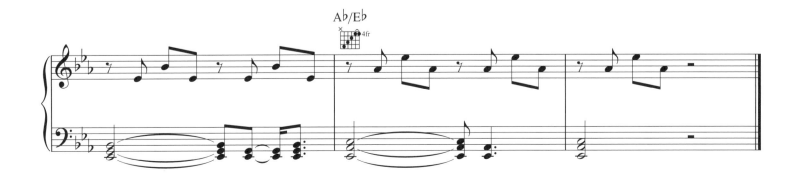

SCARED TO BE LONELY

Words and Music by GEORGIA OVERTON,
GIORGIO TUINFORT, NATE CAMPANY,
MARTIJN GARRITSEN and KYLE SHEARER

ROCKSTAR

Words and Music by LOUIS BELL,
OLUFUNMIBI AWOSHILEY, AUSTIN POST,
CARL ROSEN, SHAYAA BIN ABRAHAM-JOSEPH
and JO-VAUGHN VIRGINIE

Moderate Hip Hop groove

I been fuck-in' hoes and pop-in' pill - ies, man, I feel just like a rock-star.

All my broth-as got that gas and they al-ways be smok-in' like a Ras - ta.

Fuck-in' wit' me, call up on a U - zi and show up, man, them the shot - tas.

SHAPE OF YOU

Words and Music by ED SHEERAN,
KEVIN BRIGGS, KANDI BURRUSS,
TAMEKA COTTLE, STEVE MAC
and JOHNNY McDAID

SIGN OF THE TIMES

Words and Music by HARRY STYLES,
JEFF BHASKER, ALEX SALIBIAN,
TYLER JOHNSON, MITCH ROWLAND
and RYAN NASCI

SLOW HANDS

Words and Music by NIALL HORAN,
JOHN HENRY RYAN, ALEXANDER IZQUIERDO,
RUTH-ANNE CUNNINGHAM, TOBIAS JESSO JR.
and JULIAN BUNETTA

SORRY NOT SORRY

Words and Music by DEMITRIA LOVATO,
SEAN DOUGLAS, WARREN FELDER,
WILLIAM SIMMONS and TREVOR BROWN

SILENCE

Words and Music by KHALID ROBINSON
and MARSHMELLO

STAY

Words and Music by ALESSIA CARACCIOLO,
ANDERS FRØEN, JONNALI PARMENIUS,
SARAH AARONS, ANTON ZASLAVSKI
and LINUS WIKLUND

SOMETHING JUST LIKE THIS

Words and Music by ANDREW TAGGART,
CHRIS MARTIN, GUY BERRYMAN,
JONNY BUCKLAND and WILL CHAMPION

STRIP THAT DOWN

Words and Music by STEVE MAC,
QUAVIOUS KEYATE MARSHALL, THOMAS SYLVESTER ALLEN,
HAROLD BROWN, MORRIS DICKERSON, LeROY L. JORDAN,
LEE OSKAR LEVITIN, CHARLES W. MILLER,
HOWARD E. SCOTT, ED SHEERAN, LIAM PAYNE,
BRIAN DEREK THOMPSON, ORVILLE BURRELL,
RICKARDO GEORGE DUCENT and SHAUN PIZZONIA

* *Recorded a half step lower.*

Five shots in, ___ she in love now. I prom-ise when we pull up, shut the club down.

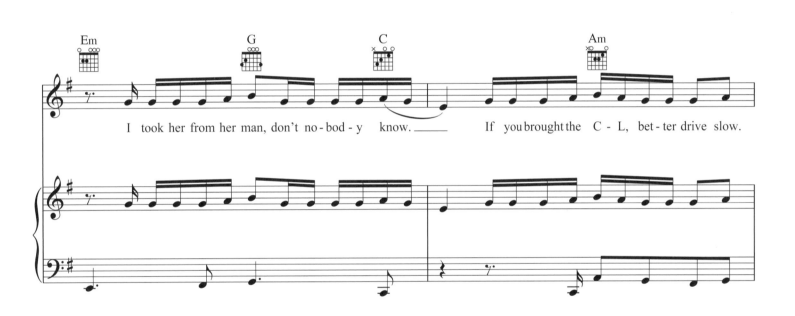

I took her from her man, don't no-bod-y know. ___ If you brought the C - L, bet-ter drive slow.

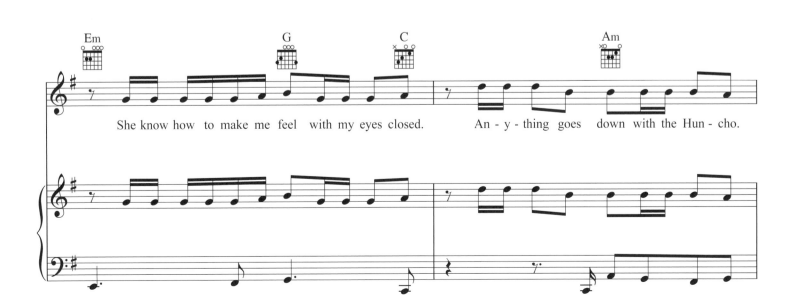

She know how to make me feel with my eyes closed. An - y - thing goes down with the Hun - cho.

THAT'S WHAT I LIKE

Words and Music by BRUNO MARS, PHILIP LAWRENCE,
JAMES FAUNTLEROY, RAY CHARLES McCULLOUGH II,
CHRISTOPHER BRODY BROWN, JEREMY REEVES,
JONATHAN YIP and RAY ROMULUS

Half-time groove

(Ey, ey, _____ ey.) I got a con-do in Man-hat-tan; ba-by girl, what's hap-p'nin'? You and your ass in-vit-ed, so gon' and get to clap-pin'. Yo, pop it for the pimp, pop,

* Recorded a half step higher.

THUNDER

Words and Music by DAN REYNOLDS,
WAYNE SERMON, BEN McKEE,
DANIEL PLATZMAN, ALEXANDER GRANT
and JAYSON DeZUZIO

Just a young gun with a quick fuse, I was up-tight, want to let loose.

I was dream-ing of big-ger things and want to leave my own life be-hind.

Not a yes sir, not a fol-low-er. Fit the box, fit the mold, have a seat in the

TOO GOOD AT GOODBYES

Words and Music by SAM SMITH,
TOR HERMANSEN, MIKKEL ERIKSEN
and JAMES NAPIER

Pop Ballad

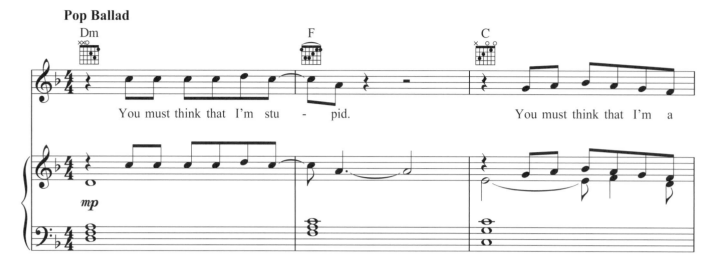

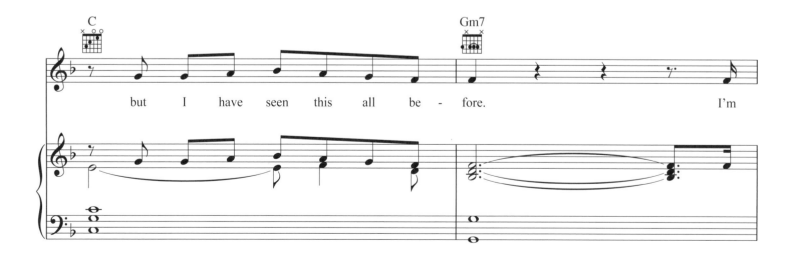

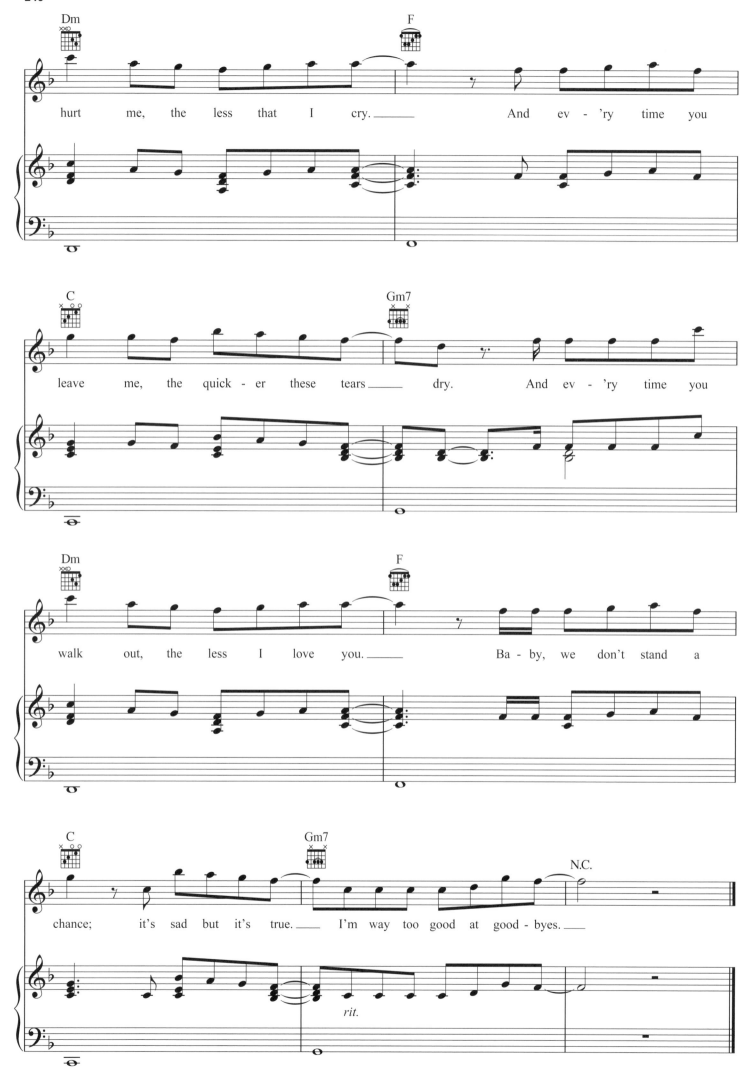

THERE'S NOTHING HOLDIN' ME BACK

Words and Music by SHAWN MENDES,
GEOFFREY WARBURTON, TEDDY GEIGER
and SCOTT HARRIS

WHAT LOVERS DO

Words and Music by ADAM LEVINE,
SOLANA ROWE, JASON EVIGAN,
OLADAYO OLATUNJI, BRITTANY HAZZARD,
VICTOR RAADSTROM and BEN DIEHL

WILD THOUGHTS

Words and Music by DJ KHALED,
BRYSON TILLER, DAVID McRAE,
JERRY DUPLESSIS, MARVIN HOUGH,
WYCLEF JEAN, CARLOS SANTANA,
KARL F. PERAZZO, RAUL REKOW,
JAHRON BRATHWAITE and ROBYN FENTY

A - noth - er one.

We the best mu - sic.   D - J Kha - led.

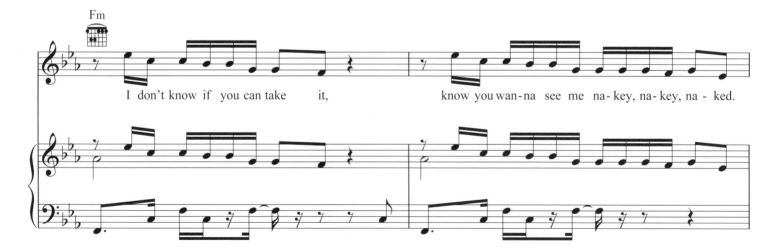

I don't know if you can take   it,   know you wan-na see me na-key, na-key, na - ked.

dia - monds ain't noth - ing when I'm shin - in' with ___ ya. Just
throw that ass back, bou - quet.

Cm

keep it white and black as if I'm ya sis - ter,
Call me and I can get it jui -

I'm too hip to hop a - round town out here with ___ ya.
cy, I can tell you're gone off the D'us -

1.

Fm

I know I ___ get wild, wild, wild.

WOLVES

Words and Music by SELENA GOMEZ,
CARL ROSEN, ANDREW WOTMAN,
ALI TAMPOSI, LOUIS BELL
and MARSHMELLO

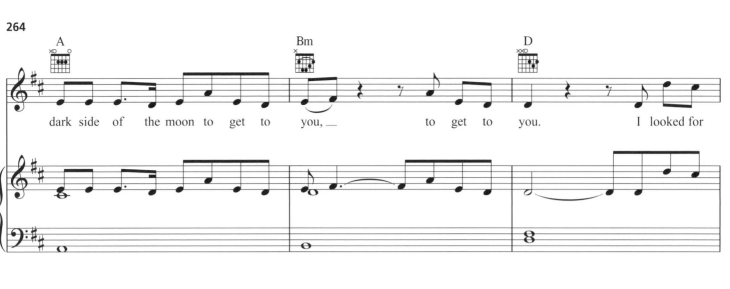

dark side of the moon to get to you, __ to get to you. I looked for

love in ev - 'ry stran-ger, took too much to ease the an-ger, all for you, __ yeah, all for

you. I been run-ning through the jun - gle, I been cry-ing with the wolves to get to

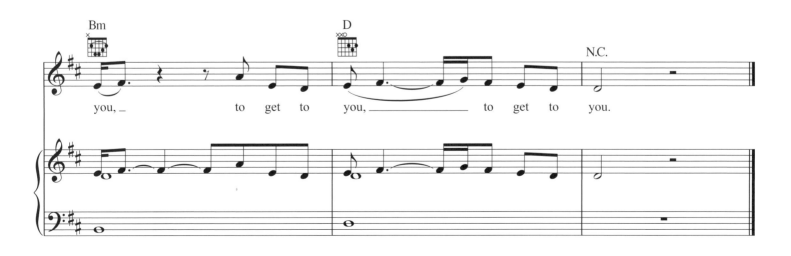

you, __ to get to you, __ to get to you.

2U

Words and Music by JUSTIN BIEBER,
DAVID GUETTA, JASON BOYD,
GIORGIO TUINFORT and DANIEL TUPARIA

Fast, driving beat

No lim-it in the sky__ that I won't__ fly__ for you.
Cu-pid in a line,__ ar-row got your name__ on it.

Oh,____ yeah.__

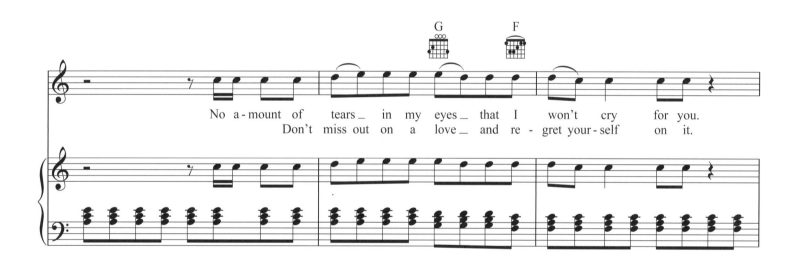

No a-mount of tears__ in my eyes__ that I won't cry__ for you.
Don't miss out on a love__ and re - gret your-self__ on it.

Oh,____ no.__
Oh._____

With ev - 'ry breath__ that I take,__
O-pen up your mind,__ clear your head,__

* Recorded a half step lower.

YOUNG, DUMB AND BROKE

Words and Music by KHALID ROBINSON,
JOEL LITTLE and TALAY RILEY

Moderately slow

Recorded a half step lower.